Sheep In The Sky

By Bakthi Ross

The cloud shapes are real photographs taken by Bakthi Ross.

Author

Bakthi Ross

Copyright © 2017

ILLUSTRATED BY BAKTHI ROSS
(Pictures are illustrated with an optical mouse)

ISBN 978 1 922220 23 3

Cloud Shapes

Cloud Shapes

A clear sky. Clouds slowly formed.

They moved slowly.

Then there were slow and medium whirly winds,

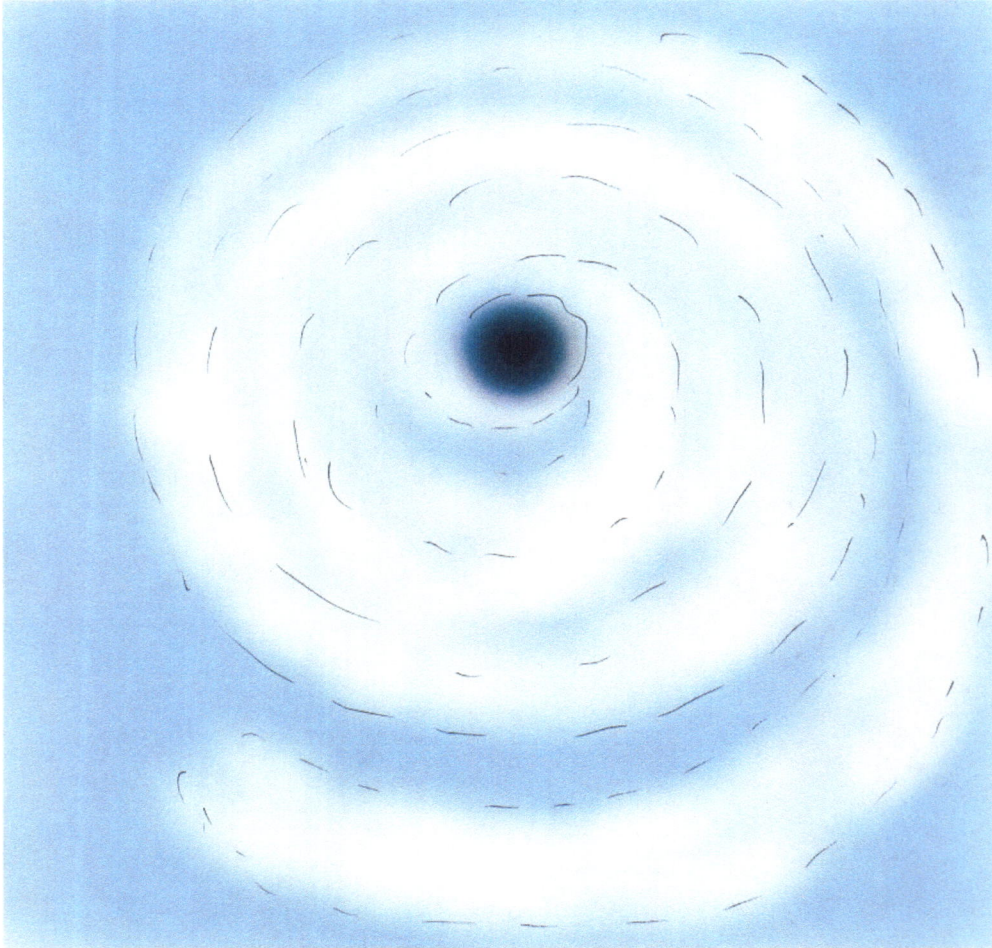

and a big strong cyclone wind.

All were blowing above the earth.

First one to chase the clouds was slow whirly wind. It made many shapes of clouds, like the lumpy wool, flat smoke, rocket smoke, long clouds and fat clouds.

Wind moved the little clouds and made gentle showers.

The medium whirly wind made many shapes of clouds. There were sheep chasing after each other.

There was a dog paddling.

Giraffe moving.

Duck waddling.

Rabbit hopping.

Fox trailing.

Goose flying.

Crocodile sleeping.

The wind moved the dark clouds and made thunder storms.

In late spring the wind made rainbows.

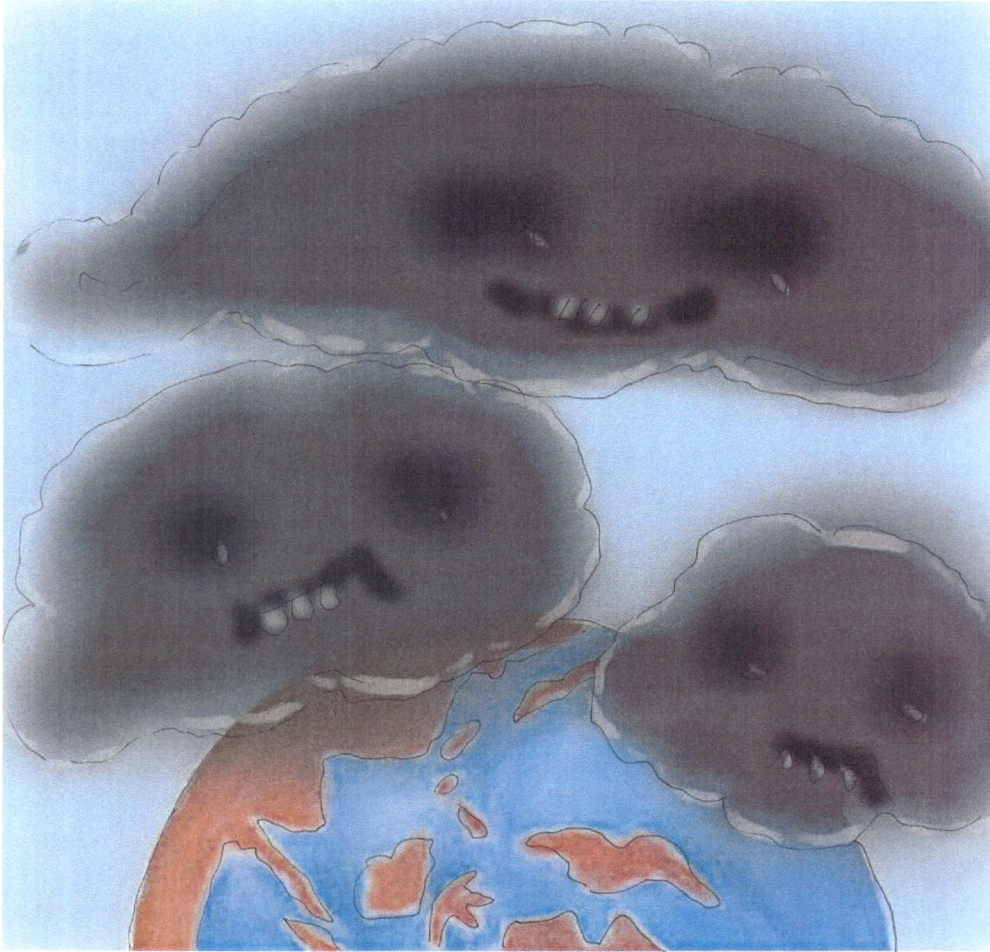

Finally came the strong cyclone wind and made many shapes of dark cloud. Dark big monster shaped clouds.

Ghosts like clouds.

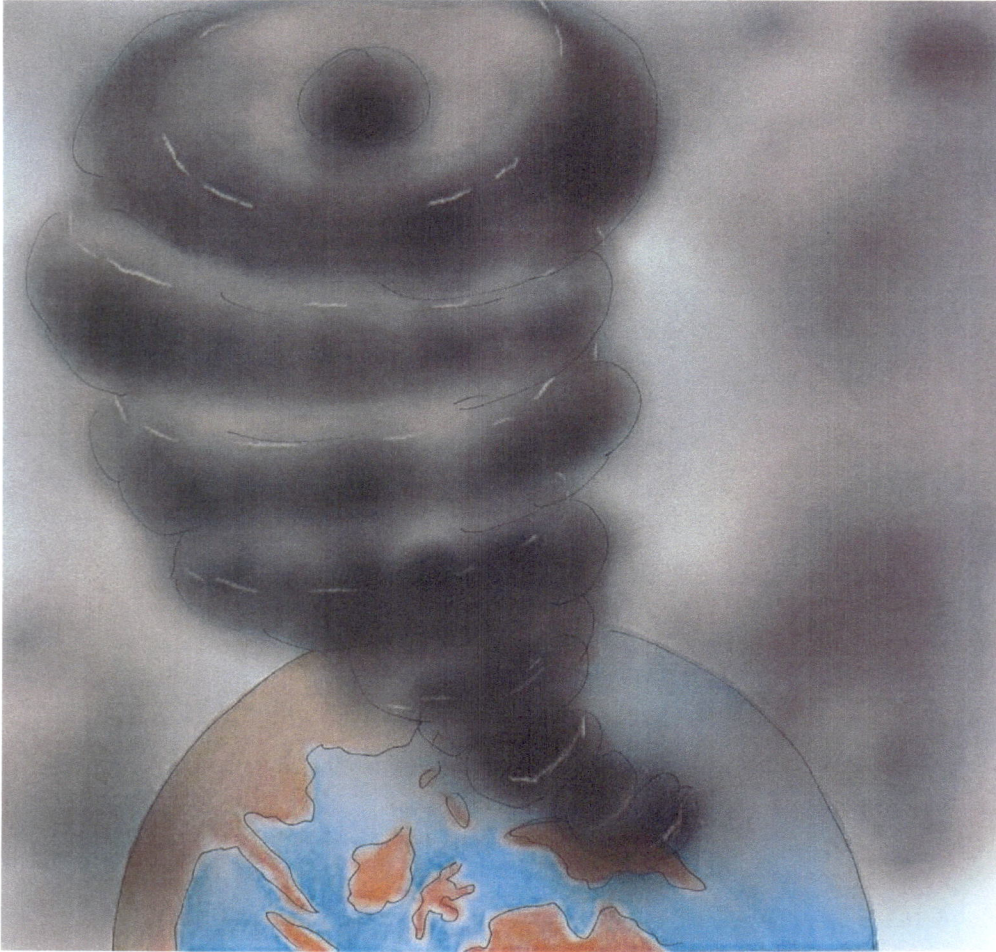

Wind made big tornado like whirls.

Wind moved the dark clouds fast, it gathered above the earth and cried.

The humans called the cyclone wind's work as a big gale. It made big thunder and lightning. It moved houses, trees and power poles. It was the scariest wind.

After the rain, the clouds disappeared for a while and clouds came again for the wind to chase.

Wind chased the clouds from hot places to cold places and cold places to hot places and made rain.

In hot places they shone with the sun.

In cold places they made snow.

Wind chased the clouds here and there and had lots of fun with the clouds.

When everything was calm and no wind blowing the clouds, clouds sat there like sheep without a shepherd.

Clouds formed bird shapes.

Birds.

A big bird in the sky.

Feathers of a bird.

A seahorse in the sky.

A jelly fish floating in the sky.

A horse on the run.

A dragon from the past.

A malee fowl.

A duck.

A fish.

A crocodile.

A fish with feathers.

A rat race.

A white swan.

Dinosaurs.

Alien birds.

Aliens!

Sheep!

A horse's head.

The Emu!

Pigs and birds.

Birds and a fish.

Long long ago a longest bird…..!

A turtle and rats.

Worms and a swan.

A giant tortoise and caterpillars.

A big duck and chicks.

Alien birds!

Birds and a fox.

A bird and a chick.

Crabs and a swan.

Alien birds!

A turtle and birds.

Visits from the aliens.

Monsters!

A crocodile and a bird.

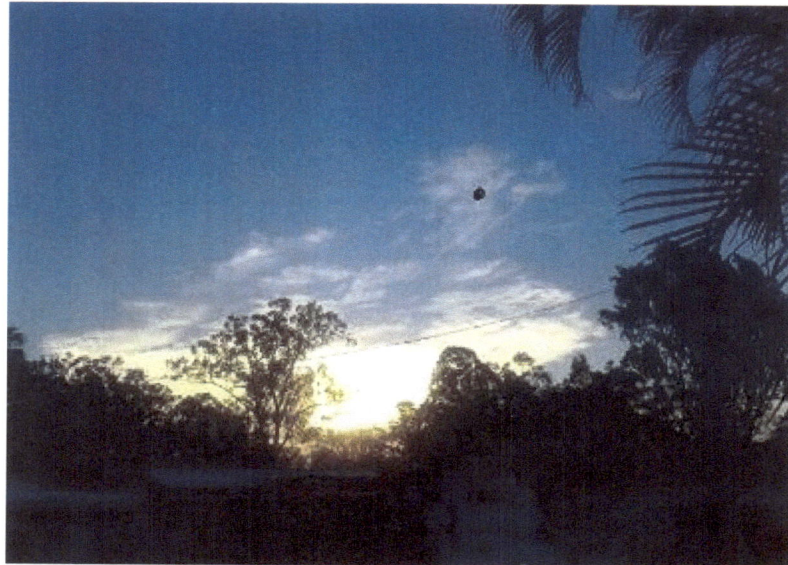

A crocodile and a bird on a nest.

Fish and a bird watch.

Pigs do fly! My! Ducks.

Cloudy aliens.

A frog, a pig and a duck.

Elephants and a cat.

A big bird and a squirrel.

Birds and caterpillars.

An emu and a rabbit.

A goat and a bird.

An elephant and a poodle.

Aliens.

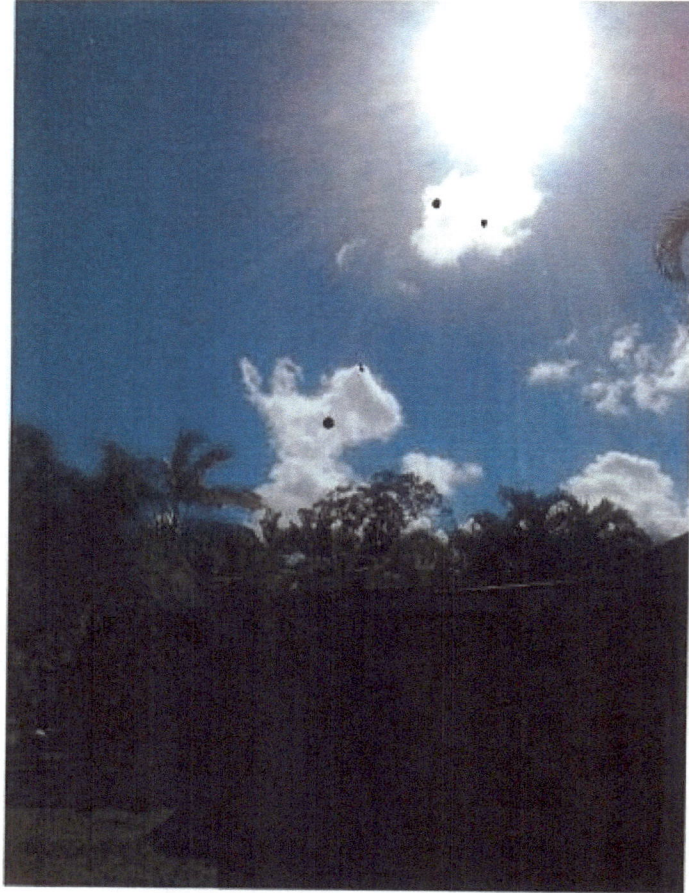

A dog and a sun turtle.

A goat and a fish.

Trails of clouds.

Big whirl and a slow whirl.

Flow of feathers.

Dark clouds.

A chicken and a weasel.

A flying bird.

Birds.

A dog and an alien.

Australia.

Cloud movements.

E for an end.

www.ingramcontent.com/pod-product-compliance
Lightning Source LLC
Chambersburg PA
CBHW060809270326

41928CB00002B/33